LAUCHIE, LIZA AND RORY

Lauchie, Liza & Rory

Sheldon Currie

Lauchie, Liza and Rory
first published 2004 by
Scirocco Drama
An imprint of J. Gordon Shillingford Publishing Inc.
©2004 Sheldon Currie
Adapted for the stage with Mary-Colin Chisholm

Scirocco Drama Series Editor: Glenda MacFarlane
Cover Design by Doowah Design Inc.
Author photo by Bernice MacDonald
Printed and bound in Canada

We acknowledge the financial support of the Manitoba Arts Council, The Canada Council for the Arts and the Government of Canada through the Book Publishing Industry Development Program (BPIDP) for our publishing program.

All rights reserved. No part of this book may be reproduced, for any reason, by any means, without the permission of the publisher. This play is fully protected under the copyright laws of Canada and all other countries of the Copyright Union and is subject to royalty. Changes to the text are expressly forbidden without written consent of the author. Rights to produce, film, record in whole or in part, in any medium or in any language, by any group amateur or professional, are retained by the author.
Production enquiries should be addressed to:
Mulgrave Road Theatre
Box 219, Guysborough, NS, B0H 1N0
theatre@mulgrave.ca
or
Sheldon Currie
1718, Rte 316
St. Andrews, NS, B0H 1X0
sheldon.currie@ns.sympatico.ca

Canadian Cataloguing in Publication Data

Currie, Sheldon
    Lauchie, Liza and Rory/Sheldon Currie.
A play.
ISBN 0-920486-59-X

I. Title.
PS8555.U74L39 2004   C812'.54   C2004-904798-1

J. Gordon Shillingford Publishing
P.O. Box 86, RPO Corydon Avenue, Winnipeg, MB Canada R3M 3S3

Acknowledgements

Many thanks to Addy Doucette, Artistic Producer of Festival Antigonish who asked me to write the play and arranged for Mary Vingoe, Artistic Director of Eastern Front Theatre, to give it a proper workshop. Thanks to Mary for teaching me how to make a play out of a short story. Thanks to Emmy Alcorn, Artistic Producer of Mulgrave Road Theatre for touring the play in Nova Scotia and beyond. And a million thanks to Mary-Colin Chisholm, the genius director, who showed everybody how two people on a stage can be as many people as they want to be.

Playwright's Notes

The characters of the play are distributed between two actors. The man plays the twins, Lauchie and Rory, the woman plays the sister Anne and the wife Liza. The man also plays Liza's Italian father. The woman also plays Rory's girlfriend/nun. The actors use body language, voice change and personal props (eg: eye glasses) to change from one character to another. The actors by turns play the mother. The mother and Lauchie and Rory are presented also as puppets (eg: human-size sticks with squares of bristle board, dressed appropriately, with a face hole for the actors to step into. Young Rory is played by the woman when he is an older student but when young is an invisible, imaginary child. The priest doing the wedding is a talking prayer book held overhead by the groom.

These devices were invented under the direction of Mary-Colin Chisholm. The written stage directions were organized by Christian Murray, based on solutions arrived at during the first two productions. The play as directed by Mary-Colin Chisholm was hilarious and had the crowds in stitches—even though it is a tragic love story.

Development History

1982 *Lauchie, Liza and Rory* appeared as a short story in *The Antigonish Review*.

1997 Festival Antigonish Artistic Director Addy Doucette invited Currie to adapt his short story for the stage. The associated script workshop included the following personnel:
Dramaturge   Mary Vingoe
Director   Mary-Colin Chisholm
Stage Manager   Mary Sadoway
Actors   Burgandy Code and Mike Petersen

The script was produced by Festival Antigonish for its Late Night Series.
Director   Mary-Colin Chisholm
Stage Manager   Mary Sadoway
Actors   Burgandy Code and Mike Petersen

2003 The script was expanded at Mulgrave Road Theatre. This full-length version toured Nova Scotia.
Director   Mary-Colin Chisholm
Stage Manager   Kirsti Bruce
Actors   Burgandy Code and Christian Murray

2004 Mulgrave Road took this revised production to the Magnetic North Theatre Festival in Edmonton.

Sheldon Currie

Sheldon Currie was born in Reserve Mines, Cape Breton, Nova Scotia, and often draws from the mining experience in his writing. His novel *The Glace Bay Miner's Museum* was adapted for film under the title *Margaret's Museum*. His other books include *The Story So Far*, *The Company Store* and *Down the Coaltown Road*. He is retired from teaching English literature at St. Francis Xavier University in Antigonish, Nova Scotia, and is writing full time.

Scene 1

ANNE sits playing solitaire. She wears glasses, these glasses denote ANNE.

ANNE: Damn damn, I did it again. Wrong king under the queen.

ANNE searches the deck, picks a red queen, substitutes.

There now. Cheat a little. Who'll know, except maybe the queen.

From off.

ELIZABETH: I'll know.

ANNE: That's my mother. She's dead. But she won't shut her mouth. She haunts me.

ANNE's mother, ELIZABETH—in picture frame on wheels—enters, played by the actor.

ELIZABETH: Start right. Or you'll end up making a mess trying to straighten it out.

ANNE: Yes, yes, yes,yes. And a mess it was. This is one sad story. But you'll enjoy it. It's kinda comical. You'll laugh your head off—because, it is sad, but it didn't happen to you. It happened to us. If it happened to your family, I'd probably laugh my head off.

ELIZABETH: Don't listen to her. She always tells tales out of school. It's none of your business. It's nobody's business.

ANNE: That's it. I can't win. I've been playing solitaire all my life. I never win.

> *ELIZABETH snubs ANNE. ANNE starts a fresh game.*

Twenty years ago. Yeah, a long story, but don't worry it won't take long. We all lived here, me, my twin brothers, identical but different as night and day, Lauchie and Rory and my mother Lizzie, say hello mother.

ELIZABETH: Anne? Why don't you just play cards and shut your big mouth?

ANNE: My mother Lizzie, God love her, was a woman of fear, and what she feared most was disgrace.

ELIZABETH: What's the good bearing children into the world, when all they ever do is expose the family to disgrace?

ANNE: Yes, we children seized on every occasion to expose the family to disgrace, the boys'd cry at baptism, that's not too bad, they'd blurt things out, like when the twins made their first confession, and the priest asked, "And do you use bad words?" Rory blurted, and loud for everybody in the church to hear—

> *Popping out of frame, to the left.*

RORY: No, I don't, but my mother does!

ANNE: That was Rory in a nutshell. Lauchie on the other hand was much less likely to expose his mother to disgrace, or if he did, it would be involuntary, like the time he farted making his first communion,

> *Becomes LAUCHIE to right of frame.*

and to make things worse, tried to blame it on Rory... Mother, remember that?

ELIZABETH: God preserve a woman alone, forced to raise, all by herself, three children, a smart alec, a solitary anchorite...

ANNE gives her mother tea.

Thank you...and a fly on the wall.

ANNE: That's me, fly on the wall. Lauchie was the solitary anchorite. My mother had a bit of a tongue on her, and a head armed with a vocabulary the size of a medieval dragon after years of playing scrabble, a game she took up in bitterness the week after my father was killed. And of course we got older, and opportunities for exposing the family to disgrace became more plentiful and more powerful. Me...

ELIZABETH: Twenty-two years old and not married. Disgraceful.

ANNE: Then twenty-three.

ELIZABETH: And not even pregnant.

ANNE: Nobody wanted to see the rest of my leg.

ANNE indicates LAUCHIE. LAUCHIE indicates his presence.

ANNE: Lauchie was, well...

ELIZABETH: Conventional.

ANNE: Neat.

ELIZABETH: Bland.

ANNE: Nice.

ELIZABETH: A bit pokey.

ANNE: Rory used to make fun of him:

RORY appears.

RORY: Lauchie, you should have been a bank robber. You wouldn't need a mask. Walk in, take the money. Nobody'd know who did it. Some nice guy with a gun and a note from his mom. You'd be rich.

LAUCHIE: Yeah. But that'd be wrong, Rory.

RORY: You got no gimp, Lauchie. No gimp.

ANNE: Rory, on the other hand, had gimp galore.

ELIZABETH: He ruined everything.

ANNE: Oh he wasn't so bad.

ELIZABETH: No just every chance he got.

ANNE: And he was funny, daring, irreverent, outrageous, depending on his mood.

RORY: *(Singing.)* Four and twenty virgins came down from Inverness. When the ball was over there were four and twenty less.

ELIZABETH: The tongue on him was enough to make you hide behind the stove with the cat.

RORY does something to illustrate ANNE's descriptions.

ANNE: They were different. Like two sides of the company house we lived in, with Lauchie's roses and hand carved wooden birds on the pickets of the fence.

ELIZABETH: Those goddamn birds.

ANNE: On our side of the front yard, and on Hughina MacDonnell's side, a yard full of gobbling turkeys and rusty car parts her husband bequeathed her when he died. But we were a family and we had happy times.

ELIZABETH: Yes. Before Rory went wild.

ANNE: Wild, for God's sake mother, he's only a show-off. Trying to get your goat.

ELIZABETH: Get my goat, get my goat. How many goats have I got to get.?He's tormented me since the day he was born, Lauchie now, he dropped like a penny, but that one came out of me arse-first with his fists clenched around my guts. I thought he was gonna turn me inside out. Still an' all he was cute.

ANNE: We had good times:

Scene 2

ANNE recalls: a lively fiddle; RORY pours drinks.

RORY: C'mon mother. Have a little nip. Wind up your bones. Slante Mhath.

ELIZABETH: Rory. You're worse than your father ever was. You know I only take a drop for my nerves. Slante Mhath.

Toast.

RORY: Take it then, or I'll get on your nerves. C'mon Anne, let's dance.

ANNE and RORY dance, walking the first part of a square dance, then the swinging part. ANNE sits.

RORY: Ni sibh dannsa Ealasaid... *(Gaelic for "Let's dance Elizabeth.")*

ELIZABETH: Oh my God. I'm too stiff.

They dance.

Oh my God I forgot how much I loved to dance, but don't kid yourself Mr. they're both gone, God and Gaelic, they're gone with the wind, they went with the farm, or should I say we left them there with the fiddle.

RORY gives her a drink from his glass.

RORY: There you go. Oil up the old joints. Swing on those old hinges.

RORY and ELIZABETH dance, same as RORY and ANNE, then sit. ANNE pulls LAUCHIE to his feet by the shirt shoulders, leads the reluctant dancer around, then fed up, sits.

Then back in present time, ANNE remembers.

ANNE: Yes. Rory fired things up when he was home.

ELIZABETH: Yes, when he wasn't careening around the countryside, knocking over mailboxes with that clunker of a car, no doubt. God knows who he travelled with, he never brought them here. I wonder why?

ANNE: You wonder why? You don't recall?

ELIZABETH: What?

ANNE: When Rory brought home his girl?

ELIZABETH: I don't want to recall, thank you.

Actor uses hand in frame to represent mouth as he exits.

A vixen, a shrew, a minx, a fur-bearing animal with a zipper up her back. Remember:

Scene 3

Flashback: Commotion on the porch. Enter RORY and KITTY, slightly tipsy, brushing off snow.

RORY: Holy mother. Cold enough to freeze the nuts off a spare tire. Here darlin', let me take your coat.

KITTY: In a minute dear, I'm too frooze. *(Whispering.)* Is

everybody asleep? Let's not wake anybody up. Sit a minute.

RORY: Sit here dear, curl up if you like. We'll have a chat.

KITTY: Oh, I just need a minute, getting late after all, and I'm off to Boston in the morning.

RORY: *(Singing.)* I took a trip to Boston for chocolate cake and frosting, but that was mighty costing, for the likes of me. Oh, herring and potatoes, herring and potatoes, herring and potatoes is good enough for me.

ANNE: *(Represented by a pair of glasses, ANNE appears from kitchen.)* Hello Rory, you likely better take a trip to bed—oh hello—

RORY: My sister Anne, Kitty.

ANNE: Hi Kitty. Rory, what happened?

RORY: Coming back from a ski trip to Ben Eoin. Ran out of gas. Mile down the road. Little too frosty to walk on to Kitty's place.

RORY becomes ELIZABETH in the frame and heads menacingly down stage right.

ELIZABETH: Well.

RORY: Kitty, this is my mother, Elizabeth.

KITTY: Hi Lizzie.

ANNE: Until that moment, only Lizzie ever called Lizzie Lizzie.

KITTY: How's she goin?

ELIZABETH: Well. Look at you. What have we here? A minx without a stole.

KITTY: Oh it's not mink dear, just rabbit.

ANNE: Until that moment only my father ever called my mother dear.

ELIZABETH: I can smell it. Thought it was dog. I didn't say mink dear, I said minx dear, and you better close it up dear, its getting frigid here, dear.

RORY: We might have to stay the night.

Actress now plays ELIZABETH and KITTY. Popping in and out of frame.

ELIZABETH: Stay. The night. Here? Where? The condition you're in. And what would people think, you two strutting off in the morning? What are you thinking?

RORY: I was thinking I live here. It's the logical place to spend the night.

ELIZABETH: When you live in a place, the custom is to spend more than the odd night in it. A home is not an inn.

KITTY: Well Mrs. MacDonald. Whatever it is, this is his home.

ELIZABETH: And who asked you?

RORY: She can curl up on the chesterfield.

ELIZABETH: She can't curl up here.

RORY: Okay. We'll curl up in the snow.

ELIZABETH: There's gas in the shed. And ye both have enough anti-freeze in the blood to see ye a mile at least.

ANNE: When Rory heard the pair of ye's, well, that sobered him up. It was the last vestige of Gaelic left on mother's tongue, Rory knew she was booting him out.

ELIZABETH: This is my house. My husband bought it from the coal company, and when he got killed he spent his

	last three days on earth here in this living room, and he left it to me.
RORY:	Okay then. Here Kitty, tie up your coat. Put my cap on.
KITTY:	Well slap my face. It was a charm to meet you Mrs. MacDonald. Underwhelming hospitality. Ta,Ta. Don't bother to make the tea.
RORY:	Sorry to bother you people. We'll take a stroll in the snow. If we do freeze don't bother to wake us, think of the disgrace.

RORY with KITTY's fur exit. ELIZABETH follows and yells after them.

ELIZABETH: Don't bring that creature here again, what's her name, Kitty, unless she brings her own litterbox.

Off or as exiting.

RORY: Fare thee well mother. And perhaps we'll see thee again someday.

ANNE: Nice work, mother. Do you think he'll ever come back after that?

ELIZABETH: I don't care if he never comes back. This is my house.

ANNE: Oh yes? And does it pay its own bills? And what if he never comes back by Friday. And by Friday, I mean payday.

ELIZABETH: Lauchie'll look after us.

ANNE: That was the worst I ever saw her. I'll never forget her eyes. Like two nickles in a plate of water.

LAUCHIE sits and gets out the Scrabble board.

It was a long time before we laid eyes on Rory, I imagine it took a month for the fire to leave his face.

It seems he was gone an eternity. Took the heart and soul of the house with him. We were left alone with Lauchie. Which was a lot like being alone.

Scene 4

LAUCHIE puts up a word on the Scrabble board.

LAUCHIE: Is heartbreak a word Annie? Annie?

ANNE: Yes, Lauchie, heartbreak is a word.

LAUCHIE: Check it. Check the dictionary.

ANNE: It's a word Lauchie.

LAUCHIE: Make sure.

ANNE: Lauchie, it's a word. Put it up.

LAUCHIE: It might be two words.

ANNE: It's a word Lauchie. It can be two, it can be one. Put it up.

LAUCHIE: Pass the dictionary.

ANNE: Lauchie!

LAUCHIE: Mmm...

ANNE: Listen. Put it up. I don't give a sweet Jesus if it's two words. It's one word.

LAUCHIE: What about heartache? I think that's one word.

ANNE gets the dictionary out and dumps it on the table.

ANNE: Here, here, here, look the goddamnn thing up. Look it up and put it up.

LAUCHIE looks up the word in the dictionary while ANNE waits.

LAUCHIE reads from the dictionary:

LAUCHIE: Heartache, grief, sorrow...

ANNE: Is it one word?

LAUCHIE: Heartbreak, deep grief, overwhelming sorrow...

ANNE: Well, is it one word? Or not?

LAUCHIE: They got a slash in the middle looks like a knife, does that means two words or two syllables?

ANNE: I don't care, put the goddamn word up.

LAUCHIE: Aahg. It's not the right word anyway.

LAUCHIE selects letter blocks and puts up a word.

ANNE: What's that...? E-M-P-T-U-R-N-I-T-Y. Empturnity! That's not a word.

LAUCHIE: It is now.

Actor uses hand in frame to represent ELIZABETH's flapping jaw.

ELIZABETH: Will you two stop that row? It's a torture. Lauchie if you want to play games for God's sake go to bingo. We could use the money, the other one gone, paycheque and all.

ANNE lays out letters on the board spelling and saying them.

ANNE: G-O-O-D-I-D-E-A

ANNE with finality puts away the dictionary and the game.

ANNE: Time for a new game Lauchie. Get to the Italian hall. Win us some money, stay for the dance. Have some fun.

LAUCHIE: I don't know Anne, I'm not lucky.

ANNE: That's in cards Lauchie. Bingo's different. If you're not lucky at bingo you might be lucky in love.

LAUCHIE: I can't play bingo.

ANNE: Just get out Lauchie, a goddamn puppet could play bingo.

> *ANNE pulls LAUCHIE up by his shirt shoulders, slams his cap on, pushes him out the door. Actor becomes ELIZABETH.*

ANNE: There. He's gone. I got him out. He'll have fun. Lighten him up.

ELIZABETH: What if he meets an Italian?

ANNE: What if he does?

ELIZABETH: You know how they like to get married.

ANNE: Mother, everybody likes to get married.

ELIZABETH: And yourself?

ANNE: The minute I meet the man. Till then, I'd just as soon live with you. At least you make your own meals and bed.

ELIZABETH: You're too fussy.

ANNE: I'm not gonna marry some galoot, just to get married and spend my life filling a pit can for some old fart in a beer belly.

ELIZABETH: One thing! If you got married, wouldn't be another paycheck out the door.

ANNE: Lauchie wouldn't leave us in the lurch.

> *Frame moves from in front of ELIZABETH to reveal LAUCHIE.*

Scene 5

LAUCHIE sits in the bingo hall studying his card.

LAUCHIE: B-15. Yes I think so. Under the B, yes... Here it is. Good, good. Now if I get the O-59, that would fill up the line. Should be good for something. What was that one—O-58...well that's no good. O-59! That's it! I think. Hey. I mean.

LAUCHIE freeze frames. LIZA appears singing "Exactly Like You."

LIZA: "I know why I'm lonesome, know why I'm blue, I'm in love with someone exactly like you."

LIZA comes over and checks the card. Yelling the numbers.

59, 51, 60, 56, 54...that's it big guy, you're the lucky man. Are you staying for the dance?

LAUCHIE: I can't dance.

LIZA: This is your lucky night. I'm a dance teacher. Come on, help with the tables, the band'll be here any minute.

LIZA and LAUCHIE move a table. A fiddle tune plays. LIZA and LAUCHIE dance parts of a square dance, walking and swinging.

The music slows into a lament. They talk.

So. What do you do?

LAUCHIE: I work in the pit, with my brother, Rory. Loading coal.

LIZA: Is that scary?

LAUCHIE: It scares our mother.

LIZA: Do you like it?

LAUCHIE: No.

LIZA: Why do you do it?

LAUCHIE: Money.

LIZA: You live with your mother?

LAUCHIE: Um-mmm.

LIZA: Your father?

LAUCHIE: Killed. In the pit.

LIZA: Let's dance. I'll teach you the fox trot.

LIZA teaches LAUCHIE the fox trot trot. He is pokey and steps on her foot.

LAUCHIE: You been teaching dancing long?

LIZA: About as long as you've been learning.

They dance in silence, getting close, comfortable. LIZA whispers something.

LAUCHIE: What did you say?

LIZA whispers.

LAUCHIE: I don't understand.

LIZA: It's Italian.

LAUCHIE: I don't speak Italian.

LIZA: This is your lucky night. I'm a language teacher. Camina means walk, mi means me, and casa means home, a means to…mi camina a casa. Repeat after me…mi

LAUCHIE: mi

LIZA: camina

LAUCHIE: camina

LIZA:	a casa
LAUCHIE:	a casa
LIZA:	Mi camina a casa
LAUCHIE:	Mi…camina…a…casa.
LIZA:	Let's go. I'll teach you the walk.

LAUCHIE and LIZA walk to her house.

LIZA:	Are you day shift this week?
LAUCHIE:	Yep.
LIZA:	There's a nice movie on.
LAUCHIE:	Is there?

At LIZA's door she turns to face him. Expectantly.

LAUCHIE:	Well then… Mmmm. Okay then. Ah, thanks for the dance lesson. And, and, the language lesson, that was good. Good night then.
LIZA:	Before you go. One more lesson.
LAUCHIE:	One more lesson. Okay.

She gets her face up close, stage whispers to his ear.

LIZA:	mi…dia…il…bacio
LAUCHIE:	Mi… I know that one.
LIZA:	Good. Mi dia… Give me.
LAUCHIE:	Mi dia…give me.
LIZA:	Il bacio. Can you guess that word?

LIZA puts her finger on her lips. Smacks.

LAUCHIE:	Bacio… A batch of something.
LIZA:	Could be, but one at a time.

LAUCHIE: What?

LIZA: Let me show you.

LIZA kisses him.

LAUCHIE: Oh. Bacio. Okay. That's good.

They kiss again.

LAUCHIE left standing, blast of romantic music, the frame is pulled in front of him, he becomes...

Scene 6

ELIZABETH: Now it's Lauchie never comes home. Did he fall in love with bingo? Is he at it every night?

ANNE: I don't think it's bingo he's at every night, mother.

ELIZABETH: Well what then?

ANNE: Well. I think he has a girl.

ELIZABETH: A girl. I was afraid of that.

ANNE: Mother, a girl is not a disgrace.

ELIZABETH: Not yet. Could be an Italian.

ANNE: Yes mother.

ELIZABETH: Didn't I tell you? These things always happen.

ANNE: What things?

ELIZABETH: How long has this been going on? What's she like, is he hiding her?

ANNE: Truth is mother dear, he was waiting for me to soften you up dear. So you wouldn't put the run on her dear.

ELIZABETH: If she shows up sober in a decent get-up, I can put up with her. I can be nice.

ANNE:	Good. Now's your chance.

Enter LAUCHIE, formal and tentative, and LIZA.

LAUCHIE:	Good evening Mother.
ELIZABETH:	Well. Good evening, Lauchie. And how are you this evening?
LAUCHIE:	Fine. I trust you had a good day?
ELIZABETH:	Yes. As a matter of fact, I did.
LAUCHIE:	Good. Good. Ah... Mother. I, ah would you, ah. Yes. Ah. I, I would like you to meet, ah, Liza, Liza Marinelli.
ELIZABETH:	How do you do, Miss... Miss Liza? Pleased to meet you.
LIZA:	Hello Mrs. MacDonald. Pleased to meet you. I've heard so many nice things about you. And you're so young.

ELIZABETH pleased with flattery.

LIZA:	And you must be Anne. How are you?
ANNE:	Oh just great. I'm young too.
ELIZABETH:	I hope you'll come visit us often.
LAUCHIE:	Good, good.
LIZA:	I hope so too.
ANNE:	And come she did.
ELIZABETH:	She did. She did. She did.
ANNE:	It was like somebody put a spark plug back in our engine.

Scene 7

LIZA: C'mon Lauchie, let's dance.

LAUCHIE: Dance teacher, teach me some more.

LIZA: Lezioni per imparare ballare.

LAUCHIE: Good, good.

> *LAUCHIE and LIZA dance. LAUCHIE clunks along.*

LIZA: See, you're getting better already.

LAUCHIE: Good, good.

LIZA: Lauchie. Ask your mother to dance.

LAUCHIE: Mother. Would you like to dance?

ELIZABETH: Oh. My joints are so stiff.

> *LAUCHIE, trying to imitate RORY's spirit, gives her a drink.*

LAUCHIE: Here mother try this. Some oil for the stiff joints.

> *They dance.*

ELIZABETH: Oh for God's sake Lauchie. I don't know what you're doing. I can't follow that step. Is that something new?

> *LIZA takes over and dances with ELIZABETH.*

LIZA: Nothing new Mrs. MacDonald. Just a fox trot. Here let me show you.

> *LIZA and ELIZABETH dance.*

ELIZABETH: Oh. You're smooth as silk dear. *(Pause.)* Liza?

LIZA: Yes.

ELIZABETH: Could you teach me to talk Italian?

LIZA: Sure. I'm a language teacher.

ELIZABETH: Are you really?

LIZA: Well, not really, really. Just a hobby I picked up lately.

ELIZABETH: I thought you were a dance teacher.

LIZA: What I really am is a hairdresser.

ELIZABETH: Go way. I've never had my hair done.

LIZA: Why should you? You got naturally curly. You can't improve on that.

ELIZABETH: I'd love to talk a foreign language.

LIZA: Italian's not foreign Mrs. MacDonald, we speak it right out in Dominion.

ELIZABETH: Call me Lizzie dear. Could I learn it, do you think?

LIZA: Pezzo di torta. Piece of cake. Why don't we start right now?

ELIZABETH: Okay. I hope it's easier than dancing.

LIZA: OK. Lizzie. Say spaghetti.

ELIZABETH: Spaghetti! Anybody can say spaghetti.

LIZA: Of course.

ELIZABETH: What's it mean?

LIZA: It means spaghetti.

ELIZABETH: You tricked me.

LIZA: No, no, we start with what we know. Now say vorrei spaghetti.

ELIZABETH: Vorrei spaghetti.

LIZA: Very good, perfect.

ELIZABETH: What's it mean?

LIZA: It means, I want spaghetti.

ELIZABETH: Really. I can say that. Vorrei spaghetti...vorrei... spaghetti...vorrie...macaroni...vorrie lasagna ...vorrei Kraft Dinner.

Scene 8

> *Blast of romantic music. LAUCHIE, arms in the air.*

LAUCHIE: Bingo!

> *He begins to embrace Liza in slow motion but bumps his chin soundly into her eye. Transition.*

Scene 9

> *LAUCHIE and LIZA on the walk home.*

LAUCHIE: I think tonight's the night.

LIZA: What do you mean?

LAUCHIE: I think I could do it tonight.

LIZA: What are you talking about?

LAUCHIE: Tell them.

LIZA: Tell them?

LAUCHIE: Yes, yes, tell them.

LIZA: Tell them what?

LAUCHIE: Well, should we tell them we're engaged?

LIZA: Oh. Are you sure? Are we engaged? You're just up in the air with the bingo money.

LAUCHIE: I know, I know. But that's it, now we got the

	money. We can do it, we can do it. Are you worried Liza?
LIZA:	No I'm not worried, but where will we live?
LAUCHIE:	Well Hughina's gonna soon move out from next door. I'll put in for it now we got the bingo money.
LIZA:	You're sure?
LAUCHIE:	We should do it, let's go home and do it.
LIZA:	Let's go to my house first, Papa's not home.

LIZA seductively leads LAUCHIE off.

Scene 10

Actor plays ELIZABETH.

ELIZABETH:	You two are back early. They cancel bingo? Did hell freeze over?

LAUCHIE is tongue tied.

LIZA:	Lauchie?
LAUCHIE:	Well…it's early. We left early, we, ah, well, the thing is…
LIZA:	We won five hundred.
ELIZABETH:	Oh my god!
LAUCHIE:	We left early. We had to, we needed to, yes, well.
LIZA:	We went to Biancini's for tea and chips. And…

LIZA looks expectantly at LAUCHIE.

LAUCHIE:	And, ah, we had tea and chips.
LIZA:	We decided something.
LAUCHIE:	Yeah, yeah we did, we decided.

ELIZABETH: For god's sake Lauchie you're as nervous as a cat at the dog's dish...what is it?

RORY enters, singing. Not seeing LIZA but LIZA seeing him.

RORY: The village prostitute was there, she had the crowd in fits / leaping from the chandelier and landing on her...

ANNE: Of course Rory had to pick that moment to lurch back into our lives, crippled from a ski accident, half drunk, a bottle of rum in one hand, a broken ski in the other.

RORY: Well Lauchie b'y, I'm gonna tell ya, ya shoulda come skiing to Ben Eoin, quite the time, quite the time. Ya coulda got your wick dipped there b'y.

ANNE: For God sake Rory, mind your tongue, and don't be so foolish.

Actress becomes ELIZABETH.

ELIZABETH: Foolish! It's worse than foolish. Irresponsible. He's not satisfied the pit doesn't kill him, like it did his father, he has to go flying down hills half drunk trying to kill himself.

RORY: C'mon Lizzie, you can do better than that. Use your scrabbled brain. Get out your scrabbled dictionary and lay me low.

ELIZABETH: I don't need a dictionary to lay you low mister. Off on a tear for three months: irresponsible covers it, but other words come to mind you besmeared and besotted wretch, you reprehensible, malignant wreck, you are deficient, defective, deplorable, detestable, not to mention drunk—and that's just the D's.

RORY takes a slug of rum. LIZA, unnoticed by RORY, is amused by the following speech:

RORY: Way to go, Lizzie, but listen here dear, I apologize. In the future I will try to be responsible...and testable, and plorable, and fective, and ficient...

ELIZABETH: How about sober?

RORY: How's bout "runk"?

ANNE: Mother couldn't resist that last shot, and of course, Rory wouldn't let her have the last word, on top of an apology, but we knew she was pleased, even if it was a backhanded apology. She was glad he was home.

RORY looks around. Sees LIZA:

RORY: Oh! So who are you?

LAUCHIE: Ah. Rory, I'd ah... I'd like you to meet, ah, Liza...

They shake hands.

LIZA: I've heard a lot about you Rory. Pleased to meet you at last.

They shake hands. LIZA bends her knee in a slight curtsy or genuflection under the pressure of RORY's hand. They continue to hold hands.

RORY: Hello Liza.

Singing Jimmy Rogers's "Liza" song, he begins to swing dance with his bad leg. She joins in.

Pleased to meet you. I haven't heard a thing about you. Keeping you to himself is he?

LIZA peels RORY's hand from hers, finger by finger, as if peeling a banana, caressingly, with feigned impatience (or something like that). When she withdraws her hand, RORY leaves his hanging in the air. ELIZABETH watches warily.

ANNE: I couldn't believe my eyes. Even before they met Liza was gawking at him, laughing at his tomfoolery. Mother noticed it too.

LIZA: Elizabeth, how do you tell them apart?

ELIZABETH: Without their clothes on they're like two knives on a plate, but once you get to know them, you'll know them.

ANNE: My heart sank, I could see the minute Liza laid eyes on Rory, she knew she'd made a mistake.

ELIZABETH: So Lauchie, Liza, what were you talking about before we were so rudely interrupted?

LIZA: Well, well.

LAUCHIE: We're engaged.

ELIZABETH: Oh my God. What will we live on. I mean, where will you live?

LIZA: Well. I think we're going to live here.

ELIZABETH: Here! Here! You can't live here.

RORY: Of course you can. You'll love it here. Every night you have your choice of games, scrabble, forty five, cribbage, solitaire...lots of fun.

LAUCHIE is gaining confidence and spirit.

LAUCHIE: Not here. Not here. We'll not be living here.

LIZA: Hughina MacDonnell's movin' out, she's gonna live with her daughter.

LAUCHIE: I'm putting in for her place, Hughina—next door. Funny eh. Next door. Same house but different eh. Two houses, exactly the same on the outside, but quite different inside. Like you and me eh, Rory, quite different on the inside. *(LAUCHIE puts his arm around LIZA and gives her a hug.)* Quite different, eh Liza?

LIZA is startled by the question and recovers quickly by answering, in a panic, a question not yet asked. Actor transitions behind LIZA alternating LAUCHIE and RORY, a devil/angel.

LIZA: Oh... We don't know when, yet. Her daughter is adding on to her house... We have to wait.

RORY winks.

Scene 11

Jimmy Rogers's "Liza" song plays, ELIZABETH dusts frame and herself. ANNE enters with tea they begin to play Scrabble. ELIZABETH struggles to place tiles on stand, eventually manages to sit with frame.

ELIZABETH: Annie?

ANNE: What?

ELIZABETH: What do you think of Liza?

ANNE: I think she's nice.

ELIZABETH: I think she's nice myself. That's not what I mean.

ANNE: What do you mean Mother?

ELIZABETH: You know what I mean.

ANNE: Why don't you just tell me?

ELIZABETH: Do you think she has to get married?

ANNE: I think she ought to get married, but I wonder who should she marry.

ELIZABETH: That's what I mean. Is she the right girl for Lauchie?

ANNE: I don't know if Liza is the right woman for Lauchie. But is Lauchie the right man for Liza. I'm gonna tell her to make up her mind. This is no time to wait.

ELIZABETH: Don't you dare.

ANNE: Why not?

ELIZABETH: Think of the talk. Scandal.

ANNE: What are you talking about?

ELIZABETH: Look. Rory has his pick of women. He drops them as fast as he pick's them up. Think about that. How would that look? Where would Lauchie turn? I think she'd be better off.

ANNE: And you—and me. We'd be better off.

ELIZABETH spells a word on the board. ANNE reads the letters.

ANNE: G-u-d-e-n-u-f.

ELIZABETH: Gudenuf, gudenuf.

Exits.

ANNE: So I didn't say a word. God forgive me. I didn't say a word. The courtship clunked along, with Rory clowning around the edge of it, acting the gawk, hoping against hope.

ANNE reads from her diary.

ANNE: Then all of a sudden, Rory gave up. I didn't know why till later. I did know that Liza had taken to going down to the pit and walking Lauchie home.

Scene 12

A miner in a black miner's helmet emerges. LIZA approaches.

LIZA: Lauchie?

RORY pretends to be LAUCHIE.

RORY: Hello.

LIZA: How'd it go today?

RORY: Today. Oh it went well today. Well, you know, ah, we had a little flooding, awful wet, awful wet, but, ah, we cleaned it up, mostly, had to leave Rory behind to finish up.

LIZA: Aren't you going to kiss me?

They embrace and a LAUCHIE kiss turns into a RORY kiss.

Lauchie.

They kiss again. They stop kissing.

Lauchie!

RORY: Rory.

She pulls away

LIZA: Rory where's Lauchie?

RORY: He's still in the pit, he wanted to work an extra shift.

LIZA: Why, why did you trick me?

RORY: I'm just teasin'.

LIZA: That's cruel.

RORY: It just happened Liza, but we should talk, you know how I feel.

LIZA: It's too late.

RORY: Too late?

LIZA steps back, puts her hand on her belly.

LIZA: It's too late.

He approaches, LIZA slaps RORY.

It's too late.

Scene 13

Actor plays an ancient PAPA, walking up the isle, to give away LIZA, sees the twins, is confused, grabs the groom (mime) wrong one, grabs LAUCHIE. PAPA transforms to LAUCHIE. LIZA holding bouquet and Bible. Bible is handed off to actor, they turn upstage, the Bible is a puppet priest. He looks down over couple.

PRIEST: Dear friends in Christ. You are about to enter into a union, sacred and serious, established by God himself, thus giving to man and woman a share in the work of creation, the work of continuing the human race. In this way he sanctifies human love and enables men and women to help each other to live as children of God, sharing a common life. This union will bind you together for life in an intimate relationship that will affect your future with its hopes and disappointments, successes, failures, pleasures, pains, joys, sorrows, all of them now hidden from your eyes.

ANNE: I don't know how they felt, but that speech sure scared the hell out of me.

PRIEST: Do you Lauchie take Liza for your lawful wedded wife?

LAUCHIE: I do.

PRIEST:	Do you Liza take Lauchie for your lawful wedded husband?
LIZA:	I do.
PRIEST:	I call upon all here present to witness this holy union. Man must not separate what God has joined together.
ANNE:	The priest sounded like a carpenter nailing shut a door. I waited for him to say:
PRIEST:	If anyone knows any reason why this couple should not be married, speak now or forever hold your peace.
ANNE:	I forgot the priest only says that in movies, and I waited, my brain and my heart screaming in the silence.

LAUCHIE places ring on finger almost breaking it in doing so. They face audience, wedding picture pose. The Wedding March plays. LIZA throws bouquet, ANNE catches it, drops it in shock, kicks it off stage.

After the wedding, mother dropped dead.

She knocks the frame over. Caught by RORY.

Mission accomplished, I guess. Rory found her.

RORY:	Well, my God Mother, yes it was bad enough but you didn't have to turn it into the end of the world.

Scene 14

RORY:	Dies Irae, dies illa/ Solve saeclum in favilla...etc.
ANNE:	And of course it was Rory who sang at the Mass. He had to, she put it in her will. Which made Lauchie as cross as a wet cat, because she always

made out that he was her favourite. I guess death is like rum, the truth comes out in it.

The puppet priest conducts the funeral service.

PRIEST: De profundis clamo ad te, Domine. Out of the depths I cry to you, Lord.

LAUCHIE
and ANNE: Audi, vocem meam. Lord hear my voice.

PRIEST: Requiem aeternam dona ei, Domine. Eternal rest grant onto her O Lord.

LAUCHIE
and ANNE: Et lux perpetua luceat ei. And let perpetual light shine upon her.

Violin plays as a lament: "I Know Why I'm Lonesome." Which will be sung next in ANNE's imagination.

Scene 15

ANNE: So Hughina MacDonell moved out next door and Lauchie and Liza moved in. And every day after that, I heard her singing that lonesome song, I couldn't get it out of my head.

LIZA: I know why I'm lonesome/ I know why I'm blue/ I'm in love with someone/ Exactly like you.

ANNE: Once they settled in we all tried to be good neighbours. We even tried to play cards like a set of ordinary couples.

The actor and actress sit at either side of the up stage corner of the table. And transition with cards in each of their hands. RORY has cards in right hand; LAUCHIE in left; ANNE, cards in right; LIZA in left. The couples, look across at one another when they are addressing each other directly. From the audience point of view they are not looking at each other.

ANNE: I sat across from Rory. Liza sat across from Lauchie.

They play Auction Forty-five.

Your bid, Lauchie.

LAUCHIE: Oh. My bid. Oh. Well. Umm. Poor hand. Umm. Hand like a foot. Umm...

ANNE: Bid Lauchie. Or pass. Do something.

LAUCHIE: Umm... Fifteen.

RORY: Why in the name of God would anybody bid fifteen! Lauchie as a card player you're a good miner—twenty.

LIZA: Sixty for a hundred and twenty.

LAUCHIE: What are you doing Liza? Have you got the five and jack, have you got the ace of hearts, I have nothing in my hand, why do you think I bid fifteen?

LIZA: No talking across the table.

LAUCHIE: It's not for you to say that.

LIZA: Well I'm saying it. And I'm doing it. I'm taking a chance and I'm hoping someone will back me up. And I'm not looking for a lot of lip. If I make it we win, If I don't we're in the hole and we'll just have to find some way to crawl up out of it.

ANNE: I'll hold it. Hold sixty for a hundred and twenty.

RORY: 'At a go Annie. We'll go down in flames together, like two spitfires.

ANNE kicks RORY.

RORY: Ouch! (*Swear.*)

ANNE: Behave yourself!

RORY: Why, what's wrong with me? What's wrong with me, Liza?

LIZA: We all know what's wrong with you but knowing's not doing.

ANNE: Oh, he'd behave himself if I was there to kick him when he needed it. But it'd be hard on the shoes.

LAUCHIE: What's wrong with you Rory, what's wrong with you?

LIZA: Oh Lauchie, we're having fun.

LAUCHIE: For the love of Pete, Liza, don't be laughing at him. It makes him worse.

LIZA: Oh don't mind him, he's just joking. He's just trying to get up your nose.

LAUCHIE: Yeah well he is.

LIZA: Is he ever. And he's pulling on the hairs up there too. Wha.

RORY: I'm gonna need a drink for this. Do you want one? You can have rum and coke or coke and rum. It comes with or without ice.

ANNE: No, not for me. And don't bring it in here, if we get started we'll be into it all night.

RORY: Well it might help.

ANNE: Yeah and it might hurt.

RORY: Well I'm already hurt.

> *Three quick rounds of cards are played, each character plays.*

ANNE:	We never took a trick.
LAUCHIE:	Lucky in cards, lucky in love, eh Liza.

> *LIZA cries. LAUCHIE goes to touch LIZA's hand, she pulls away, stands.*

LAUCHIE:	What's wrong Liza?
LIZA:	Thank you Anne. We better go home.

> *LIZA exits behind LAUCHIE, he watches her ghost image exit upstage.*

ANNE: And that was the end of games. Except of course for solitaire. They lived across the wall from us. Liza was a good wife, and when little Rory was born she was a good mother. And she and I would meet at the clothesline and chat over our fence. And Lauchie and Rory were buddies in the pit and never got killed or even hurt.

> *Bird carving bit.*

And Lauchie carved birds to put on the top of his picket fence, and planted roses, after we ate the turkeys that Hughina left behind. We all sighed every day. We looked out the window and sighed. When young Rory was born we became mother and father and aunt and uncle, and Rory and I became godfather and godmother.

> *The puppet priest (actress) performs the baptism. They stand around the baptismal font. The baby, screeching his head off, is held by LIZA.*

Scene 16

PRIEST: Give the baby to the godfather.

> *LIZA gives the baby to RORY. The baby suddenly stops crying.*

PRIEST: I place my hand on the baby's chest. Pax vobiscum. Peace be with you. Quo nomine vocaris? What is your name...Rory?

RORY: What?

PRIEST: Answer for the boy. You're the godfather. Answer the question. What is the boy to be called?

RORY: The name is Roderick. But we'll call him Rory.

PRIEST: I place salt on your forehead Roderick. Accipie sal sapientia. Accept this salt of wisdom.

RORY: Watch out for the eyes there Father. Don't blind the little bugger.

PRIEST: I pour water on your forehead, Roderick. Ego te baptizo in nomine patris. I baptize you in the name of the Father.

RORY: That'll do Father, don't drown the little bugger.

PRIEST: Favete linguis Rory.

RORY: What does that mean?

PRIEST: It means, shut your mouth.

RORY: No need to get testy. I have to watch out for the boy, I'm the godfather. Just getting in a little practice.

PRIEST: Anne, take this candle, hold it up, Rory, you light it. Here's a match.

ANNE holds up the candle and RORY lights it.

Accept this burning light and keep the grace of baptism throughout a blameless life. Vade in pace. Wrap him up and take him home.

They break off the ceremony. RORY whispers to the priest.

RORY: Drop over for a little nip Father.

ANNE: We had a subdued little party to celebrate the birth and the baptism. Mother came back from the dead and danced with the priest, who wasn't there either.

Mother and priest puppets dance.

Scene 17

ANNE: Well little Rory cried for two years.

ANNE and LIZA hang clothes on the lines.

When he stopped, Liza started. Both our stairs went up the wall that separated us and I first heard her through that wall, sitting on her stairs, sobbing. We lived our subdued lives. Liza and Lauchie in their side of the house and we in ours. The years crawled. Young Rory grew like a weed with legs in our back yards.

ANNE and LIZA hang clothes on the lines. A ball rolls on stage. Young RORY, the invisible boy, plays in the sheets hanging from ANNE's line.

LIZA: Get out of there. Get him out of there. Anne.

ANNE's voice.

ANNE: Who?

LIZA: Young Rory.

ANNE: Where?

LIZA: He's into your sheets. He'll pull them in the dirt. He's worse than his uncle. Get out of there, Get.

YOUNG RORY: Vorrei gelato, per favore.

LIZA: Non...nienye. Go play ball with uncle Rory. He'll

	take you for an ice cream when he gets tired.
	LIZA throws ball off stage.
ANNE:	Where's Lauchie, Liza?
	Ball flys on stage followed by RORY.
RORY:	Atta go b'y. Drift her in there buddy. Good one, she stayed in the air almost all the way. Here you go now, keep your eye on it.
	RORY mimes easy underhand pitch.
LIZA:	Where's Lauchie? Where d'ya think? Out front carving birds. Soon there won't be a picket fence in Glace Bay without a flock of Lauchie's birds on it. We got more swallows in our attic than go back to Capistrano.
	LIZA sings "Capistrano" beautifully, followed by ANNE singing poorly.
ANNE:	Liza was always putting songs in my head. I had to sing it a hundred times out loud to get rid of it. "When the swallows come back to Capistrano/ I'll be coming back to you." I hate folding sheets. Rory, come help me fold these sheets.
	RORY and ANNE fold the sheet while ANNE narrates.
ANNE:	Just before he started school the boy stayed with us while they went to Halifax. Lauchie had to see a doctor.
	A knock on the door.
LIZA:	We're off. He's not in a good mood. You be a good boy now.
	Actress performs the voice of YOUNG RORY.
YOUNG RORY:	I don't want to be a good boy. I wanna go to

	Halifax. I want to get my lungs looked at too.
LIZA:	Rory will take you downtown.
YOUNG RORY:	I went downtown last week. I got a stupid little ice cream.

RORY lifts (Pantomime.) YOUNG RORY to his shoulders.

RORY: It's not much of a town buddy, but the circus lands tomorrow.

YOUNG RORY: The Circus!

Scene 18

Merry go round music.

Pantomimed and to music RORY and ANNE hold YOUNG RORY on a horse.

Pantomime: RORY and ANNE and YOUNG RORY on the ferris wheel.

ANNE: Rory, win a teddy bear at the duck shoot, and let's go. Shopping tomorrow.

RORY: You shoot, buddy. I'll hold it steady.

YOUNG RORY fires off a shot.

RORY: Hey. That's one dead duck.

YOUNG RORY: Hey, look, a tiger.

ANNE: Wow. A big one too.

YOUNG RORY: What do they eat?

RORY: They eat little boys if their godfather is not with them.

Circus music fades.

ANNE: The two Rorys spent the miners' vacation doing everything. They went fishing…

RORY and YOUNG RORY fish off the wharf.

RORY: Careful don't tumble off the wharf. Stand back.

YOUNG RORY: I got one! I got one!

RORY: Let me help you reel it in. Oh, a dandy, looka that, four inches long at least. Let me get the hook out.

YOUNG RORY: Can we eat it?

RORY: No, no, better not.

YOUNG RORY: Why not?

RORY: The harbour's full of shit.

YOUNG RORY: Okay.

RORY spots ALPHONSE and calls to him.

RORY: Hey Alphonse, you going out? Can we come? C'mon buddy, we'll get some mackerel, maybe a couple lobster.

ANNE resumes the narration.

ANNE: They landed with a bag of mackerel, sold them on the way home for 10 cents each, and two lobsters and an aquarium.

RORY: Let me help you now. Grab them by the back so they can't grab you.

They drop the lobsters into the tank and stand back to look.

Look at that. Nice contented family.

YOUNG RORY: Are they brothers, Uncle Rory?

RORY: Who knows. They could be twins, could be sister and brother, husband and wife. If they have a baby we'll know.

YOUNG RORY: Can you tell if it's a boy or a girl?

RORY: They're a bit like Scots b'y, you don't know lest you peek up their kilts.

YOUNG RORY: Let's take a peek.

RORY: Let's wait 'til they know us better.

ANNE and YOUNG RORY in a store.

ANNE: We all went shopping. This store has the best caps in town. Here's one like Uncle Rory's. Try it. Look at that, perfect. We got two Rory's in two Rory caps. Let's go buy a kite.

They leave the store while ANNE narrates.

ANNE: They went kite flying:

RORY: Watch her boy, she's gonna dive.

RORY helps with the string.

RORY: You got her in the nick 'a time. She nearly nose-dived into the ocean. She's steady now.

YOUNG RORY: Uncle Rory?

RORY: Yes lad?

YOUNG RORY: How come Mommy likes you better than Daddy?

RORY: Watch it, that could be dangerous... Pull that string, she'll dive again.

No, no, no, no, b'y, it's just, ah, your mother, your mother, ah, likes a good laugh now and again ...and, ah, I'm always acting the gawk, you know, saying funny things. She loves to laugh.

YOUNG RORY: She never laughs when she's home.

They sit in silence for a beat.

YOUNG RORY: Uncle Rory?

RORY: Yes lad?

YOUNG RORY: Are you my godfather?

RORY: Yes. Indeed I am.

YOUNG RORY: What is a godfather?

RORY: Oh. It's just that when your parents are away in Halifax, it's my job to look after ya. At your baptism I promised to help you keep away from the devil. So when the devil comes, I'll help you get away.

YOUNG RORY: How you gonna do that?

RORY: I'm gonna get you a bicycle.

The kite gets away from them, RORY joyfully gives chase.

RORY: She went right in the drink.

ANNE resumes narration.

Scene 19

ANNE: It was a fun week for the three of us like a real family. When Lauchie and Liza landed back, with a clean bill of health, young Rory wouldn't go home. Lauchie had to drag him back. In the morning he wouldn't go to school if Rory wouldn't take him. To keep the peace, he took him.

RORY: Here you take the apple, I'll take the scribbler and the pencil box. After school now you get right home...

Pointing a finger.

RORY: Home!

ANNE: Every day after school he'd land on us, sit and munch a carrot 'til Lauchie'd come and drag him home.

LAUCHIE: You know you were supposed to come straight home.

YOUNG RORY, just a voice performed by Actress.

YOUNG RORY: I forgot

LAUCHIE: You forgot! Nonsense. You forgot yesterday. And the day before. Are you gonna forget again tomorrow?

YOUNG RORY: I don't want to go home.

LAUCHIE: You can't stay here. This is not your home. They don't want you here.

YOUNG RORY: Yes they do.

LAUCHIE: Did they say so?

YOUNG RORY: No.

LAUCHIE: Then how do you know?

YOUNG RORY: I can tell.

LAUCHIE: Well I can tell you this young man, you better do what you're told, or I'm gonna warm your arse. Annie somebody better do something.

LAUCHIE exits with the struggling and pantomime YOUNG RORY.

ANNE: We locked him out. Pitiful. We played double solitaire, gritted our teeth.

ANNE and RORY play cards. We hear knocks on the doors and windows, a muffled cry.

YOUNG RORY: *(Off.)* Uncle Rory, Aunt Anne. Let me in.

RORY: I don't know how much of this I can stand.

ANNE: Get us a drink. Bring the bottle. That didn't work either.

Scene 20

LAUCHIE: Liza, is he asleep?

LIZA: Finally. He's not a happy boy.

LAUCHIE: Who is?

LIZA: Nobody. Is there nothing we can do about this?

LAUCHIE: I can't think of anything.

LIZA: Could we let him go over sometimes?

LAUCHIE: He won't come back. Then what? What else have we got?

Scene 21

ANNE and LIZA stand on either side of the picket fence that separates their back yards and hang laundry.

LIZA: Good drying day Anne.

ANNE: Yes. I think I'll do my sheets.

LIZA: Me too, if the wind doesn't change. The pit's spewing out a whack of soot, but it's going the other way.

ANNE: How's the boy doing Liza?

LIZA: Oh Anne. I'm at my wits' end. He won't do his homework. He's gonna fail again. Lauchie tries to help him, but he's so pokey. The boy won't cooperate.

ANNE: What does he say?

LIZA: He says he wants to do homework with Rory. But I don't know if I want to go through that again. It was like we didn't have a boy at all.

Silence for a beat or two.

ANNE: Try it Liza. Just let Lauchie make the rules.

LIZA: I'll ask Lauchie.

Scene 22

LAUCHIE: Rory.

YOUNG RORY: Yeah dad.

LAUCHIE: OK son this is how we're gonna do it.

YOUNG RORY: What?

LAUCHIE: OK Rory's gonna help with the homework.

YOUNG RORY: Good, good.

LAUCHIE: Right after school.

YOUNG RORY: OK.

LAUCHIE: You're home for supper.

YOUNG RORY: Can I go for tea after supper?

LAUCHIE: Alright but only for half an hour.

Scene 23

ANNE: And it was Magic. Four months later.

ANNE and LIZA at the clothesline.

LIZA: Good drying day Anne?

ANNE: Yes. I think I'll do my sheets.

LIZA:	Me too. Nice breeze today.
ANNE:	Yeah. How's the boy?
LIZA:	I saw the nun yesterday. She said, I don't know what's come over the boy.

LIZA pulls the report card from her apron pocket.

LIZA:	Have a look at his report card.

Scene 24

ANNE:	Look what the sister says.

Up stage LAUCHIE reads the same report card.

LAUCHIE:	He's kinda mouthy, but he does the work. Good, good.
ANNE:	Lauchie do you mind he's here so much?
LAUCHIE:	You know I do mind, but maybe it'll keep the boy outta the pit.
ANNE:	Well let's listen to the homework, we might as well enjoy it.

Scene 25

RORY places chair, points to it gesturing for YOUNG RORY to sit. YOUNG RORY still just a voice.

RORY:	Ridiculous Rory! A father and son are in prison without a roof and fly out on wings of feathers and wax. Where'd they get the feathers?
YOUNG RORY:	I don't know. Does it matter?
RORY:	Well if you're gonna make wings with feathers, you gotta get feathers.

YOUNG RORY: Maybe the prison had a chicken farm.

RORY: Okay. And the beeswax?

YOUNG RORY: Maybe the prison had beehives.

RORY: And the warden said, what are you guys doing, and they said, we're making a surprise for your birthday.

Actress now takes seat to play YOUNG RORY from here on in, sporting a RORY cap.

YOUNG RORY: That doesn't matter. It's a story. It doesn't have to be true. That's not what matters.

RORY: Okay. What matters?

YOUNG RORY: What matters is the meaning.

RORY: Oh really. So what does it mean?

YOUNG RORY: They escape. The father says, now son, don't fly too high, the sun will melt the wax, and you'll crash in the ocean. The boy flies too high, the wax melts, the feathers fly, and he nosedives into the ocean. Drowns.

RORY: So? What does it mean?

YOUNG RORY: What do you mean, what does it mean? It's obvious.

RORY: Is it?

YOUNG RORY: Yes it is?

RORY: Not to me.

YOUNG RORY: Are you stupid or what?

RORY: I'm stupid. Explain it to me.

YOUNG RORY: The boy should have obeyed his father.

RORY: That's ridiculous.

YOUNG RORY: It's not ridiculous.

RORY: It is. Now I think about it, it's not the story, the meaning is ridiculous.

YOUNG RORY: Well that's what it means.

RORY: That's not what it means.

YOUNG RORY: Alright, smartass, what does it mean?

RORY: If it means anything, it means the father is an old fart and his son did the right thing not paying him the least bit of attention.

YOUNG RORY: Why?

RORY: How is the boy gonna know how far he can climb if he doesn't try? You forgot your Latin b'y: per ardua ad astra, through adversity to the stars.

YOUNG RORY: But he went too far.

RORY: Yeah. But you can't know how far you can go if you don't go too far.

YOUNG RORY: But he's dead.

RORY: But that doesn't matter. It's a story. It's the meaning that matters.

ANNE: You two. Get to bed. You'll be dead in the morning.

RORY: Okay Annie.

RORY picks up the books, still sitting.

YOUNG RORY: You're wrong. Just because you're older you think you're right.

RORY: How do you know I'm wrong? How do you know what it means?

YOUNG RORY: Sister Margaret told us what it means. And she's just as old as you. She went to school with you.

RORY: So what does Sister Margaret say?

YOUNG RORY: It means obey your father, your teacher, your priest, and through your priest your bishop and the Holy Father the Pope.

RORY: Well you tell Sister Margaret for me she's full of shit.

ANNE: Your mother's here.

RORY: OK b'y, better go.

LIZA: Come to bed Rory...

LIZA and RORY look at each other.

LIZA: Thanks Rory.

LIZA and RORY head to door frames. She sings Italian lullabye. Both sigh.

Scene 26

ANNE resumes her narration:

ANNE: Young Rory brought the exams home. Rory would make high marks on them.

RORY: You know what Little R?

YOUNG RORY: What, Big R?

RORY: I'm looking at my French mark here.

YOUNG RORY: Yeah?

RORY: Pretty good eh?

YOUNG RORY: Not as good as mine.

RORY: Yeah, but you got the nun and your mother speaks Italian. I wonder if she'd teach me a little Italian, in case I want to say something to her some day.

YOUNG RORY: Well she understands English.

RORY: I know she understands English. But I like the romance languages.

YOUNG RORY: Just say it in French. I'll translate it for ya.

RORY: Oh I don't think so. Anyway, the thing is you got two language teachers; I'm pretty well on my own.

YOUNG RORY: Well. You got me. I'm your teacher.

RORY: Yeah. Well how much help is that? I'd rather have your mother. If they taught Gaelic in school we'd see who'd make the marks.

YOUNG RORY: Pog ma thon! *(Gaelic for "kiss my ass." Pronounced pock ma hawn.)*

RORY: If I'd a' known I was smart, I'd a stayed in school. I'd be the teacher now.

Scene 27

ANNE: Rory just couldn't stop showing off about it. Even with me. I'd ask him: What did you learn last night Rory?

RORY: Last night I learned the sailor loves the girl.

ANNE: And what have you got for homework?

RORY: For homework I got to learn the girl loves the sailor. But I know it already, puellam nautam amat.

ANNE: Now what would that be in Gaelic?

RORY: In Gaelic. Let's see... *(The following speech is spoken in Gaelic. Phonetically.)*

Ha goul ache a vinicher, air a halek. Ak ha goul ache a halek air a vinicher kur.

ANNE: I couldn't speak Gaelic so he didn't realize I knew enough to pick it up. The miner loves the girl. The girl loves the wrong miner. A sad story, all in all. But it could've been worse. Instead of drinking himself to death he was reading himself blind. By the time Young Rory hit Grade 12 they were yakking away in French or Latin or Gaelic. Young Rory landed one day with a big smile on and said to Rory:

Actress become YOUNG RORY.

YOUNG RORY: Il faut que tu ailles a l'ecole pour voir Soeur Margaret. In other words, get your arse down to school, Sister Margaret wants to kick it.

RORY: What's up?

YOUNG RORY: You'll see.

Scene 28

The classroom. SISTER MARGARET is writing on the board. RORY approaches her from behind.

RORY: Sister Margaret?

SISTER MARGARET: Yes. Is it Rory MacDonald?

RORY: Yes it is, it's Rory.

SISTER MARGARET: Yes. I'll be with you in a minute. Just trying to get tomorrow's lesson on the board.

She writes on the board. She turns to face RORY.

RORY: Kitty!?

SISTER MARGARET: Yes.

RORY: He said you were Margaret.

SISTER MARGARET: I am Margaret. My nun name. Sister Margaret after

>   Saint Margaret of the Isles, virgin and martyr.

RORY: You didn't used to be a saint, Kitty?

SISTER MARGARET: I know. I didn't used to be a virgin either but I am now.

RORY: Didn't you go to Boston.

SISTER MARGARET: I did. But I'm back. Nice to see you again, Rory.

RORY: I can't believe it's you. Wow. Remember the ski trip to Ben Eoin?

SISTER MARGARET: We probably shouldn't remember that right now, Rory.

RORY: Oh, why not? I like to. I remember it often. I broke my leg, remember?

SISTER MARGARET: Yes and that's not all you broke. I like to remember it too, but let's not do it together. Can you translate the Latin on the board.

RORY: Servabo me servabo te. Sure. You scratch my back, I'll scratch yours.

SISTER MARGARET: Impressive. And you a grade eight dropout.

RORY: Oh, the boy's the scholar. I try.

SISTER MARGARET: I hear you think I'm full of shit.

RORY: He told you that?

SISTER MARGARET: He tells me everything since he found out you used to be my buddy. Needless to say, I don't tell him everything.

RORY: So, you gonna rap my knuckles with your ruler, that why you got me here?

SISTER MARGARET: No. Since you didn't know it was me, I kinda felt like a spy. I wanted you to know.

RORY: So how long have you been a nun?

SISTER MARGARET: Oh quite a while now. I needed the commitment so it was either get married or this, so, I took this. How is your *dear* mother?

RORY: She's dead.

A bell rings.

SISTER MARGARET: Yes. Probably just as well. That was the bell dear, have to run. Prayers eh, never get enough of that.

RORY: Did you make the right choice?

SISTER MARGARET: Oh yes. I guess you make the choice. Then you make it right. And you?

RORY: I don't know if I made a choice yet, maybe I should.

SISTER MARGARET: Maybe you should.

SISTER MARGARET exits.

RORY leaves and walks home, singing:

RORY: I wish I were where Liza lies/ Night and day on me she cries/Oh that I were where Liza lies/On fair Kirkconnell lea...

Scene 29

ANNE, playing solitaire, resumes her narration:

ANNE: Young Rory graduated. Got the big scholarship, went off to college. We were lost. We walked around the house on pins and needles. Expecting. It happened quietly. That was Liza's way. She bided her time. Then picked the worst day of the year. November rain poured from the dreary sky. It felt like the house was filling up with invisible rain and we'd all be drowned in mid-air...

LIZA sets chair center stage.

LIZA: I took a big suitcase and a kitchen chair and sat in the downpour in the road between our two gates in my burberry and big rimmed felt hat, my back to the front doors, my hands folded in my lap.

ANNE plays a few cards.

RORY: Me and Lauchie watched her through our screen doors as she sat in the chair in the mud. Me and Lauchie. Two men, weary, coughing and hurting after a week of back shift in the pit. Peering through the screen doors, cups and saucers in hand, sipping tea. I went over to talk. What d'ya think Lauchie?

LAUCHIE: I think it's up to you now.

Pantomime: RORY goes out and after silent negotiation LIZA returns with him. He carries her suitcase and the chair. She sits on the chair in the kitchen. RORY pours a mug of tea, and tops it up with rum.

RORY: Here, Liza, have a mug of tea. Here we'll top that up with a bit of rum. Hot toddy...for your nerves. Mine too.

LIZA: I don't know if this is going to make anybody happy but myself. I can't help it.

Scene 30

ANNE: And so it was. And so it had to be. It might as well be later as sooner. Are you cross Lauchie?

LAUCHIE: There's nobody to be mad at, Annie. I'd like to be mad. But, you know, it's not Rory's fault. You know that. Same for Liza. It's not your fault. It's nobody's fault. Unless it's all our faults. We should'a fixed it up when it all started wrong. We all knew. But then. We wouldn't have Young Rory. I guess we all have to be happy about that.

ANNE: So what do we do now?

LAUCHIE: Why don't you get your things and bring them over here?

ANNE: What'll I tell them?

LAUCHIE: Tell them they got my chair. Tell them, keep it for a wedding present.

ANNE: Young Rory'll be surprised when he lands home Christmas.

LAUCHIE: I wonder, he's supposed to be smart. I don't think college will take it out of him that quick.

The End.

Glossary of Gaelic, Latin phrases in *Lauchie, Liza and Rory*

Page 15
Slante mhath. Good health (a toast or greeting) Slante=health, mhath= good
Phonetic spelling: slanche (a soft c) va

Ni sibh dannsa, Ealasaid: Let's dance, Elizabeth. (Lit: Will you do dancing, Elizabeth?)
Phonetic spelling: Ni shiv downsa Elasach. Ni= (fut. of do) sibh=you

Page 17
Ben Eoin. John's Mountain. A place name. (Lit: mountain or hill of John)
Phonetic spelling: Ben yawn.

Page 39
Dies irae, dies illa, solvet saeclum in favilla. The days of wrath, turn the people to burning ashes. (Lit: Days of wrath, those days, turn the people to burning ashes)
Phonetic spelling: Diaze ir eh, diaze illa, solvet sayclum in favilla. These are the first two lines of the Sequence in the Mass for the Dead. Gregorian Chant style.